Questions and Answers: Countries

Australia

A Question and Answer Book

by Nathan Olson

Consultant:
Frances Cushing, Research Associate
Edward A. Clark Center for Australian Studies
The University of Texas at Austin
Austin, Texas

Mankato, Minnesota

Fact Finders is published by Capstone Press,
151 Good Counsel Drive, P.O. Box 669, Mankato, Minnesota 56002.
www.capstonepress.com

Printed in the United States of America

Library of Congress Cataloging-in-Publication Data
Olson, Nathan.
Australia: a question and answer book / by Nathan Olson.
p. cm.—(Fact finders. Questions and answers. Countries)
Includes bibliographical references and index.
ISBN 0-7368-3747-7 (hardcover)
1. Australia—Juvenile literature. I. Title. II. Series.
DU96.O47 2005
994—dc22 2004010604

Summary: Describes the geography, history, economy, and culture of Australia in a question-and-answer format.

Editorial Credits

Megan Schoeneberger, editor; Kia Adams, set designer; Kate Opseth, book designer; Nancy Steers, map illustrator; Wanda Winch, photo researcher; Scott Thoms, photo editor

Photo Credits

AUSPIC/Michael Jones, 9
Bill Bachman, 15, 16, 17, 25
Bruce Coleman Inc./Daniel Zupanc, 12; Frank Krahmer, 4
Capstone Press Archives, 29 (coins and bill)
Corbis/Hulton-Deutsch Collection, 7; Paul A. Souders, 18–19; Royalty-Free, cover (background), 1
Corbis Sygma/Cixous Lionel, cover (foreground)
Folio Inc./Walter Bibikow, 11
Getty Images Inc./Adam Pretty, 23
Houserstock/Dave G. Houser, 13, 20
James P. Rowan, 21
StockHaus Ltd., 29 (flag)
TRIP/Robin Smith, 27

1 2 3 4 5 6 10 09 08 07 06 05

Table of Contents

Features

Where is Australia?

Australia is located between the Pacific Ocean and the Indian Ocean. It is the only country in the world that is also a continent. Australia is about the same size as the lower 48 states of the United States.

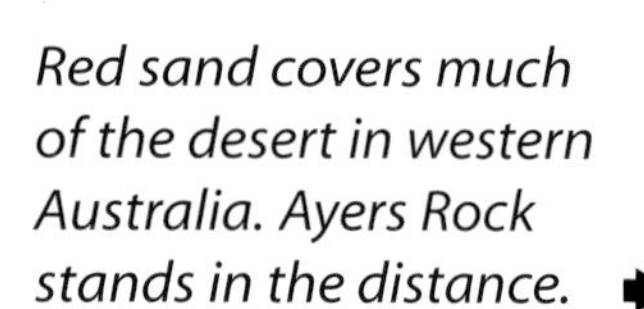

Red sand covers much of the desert in western Australia. Ayers Rock stands in the distance.

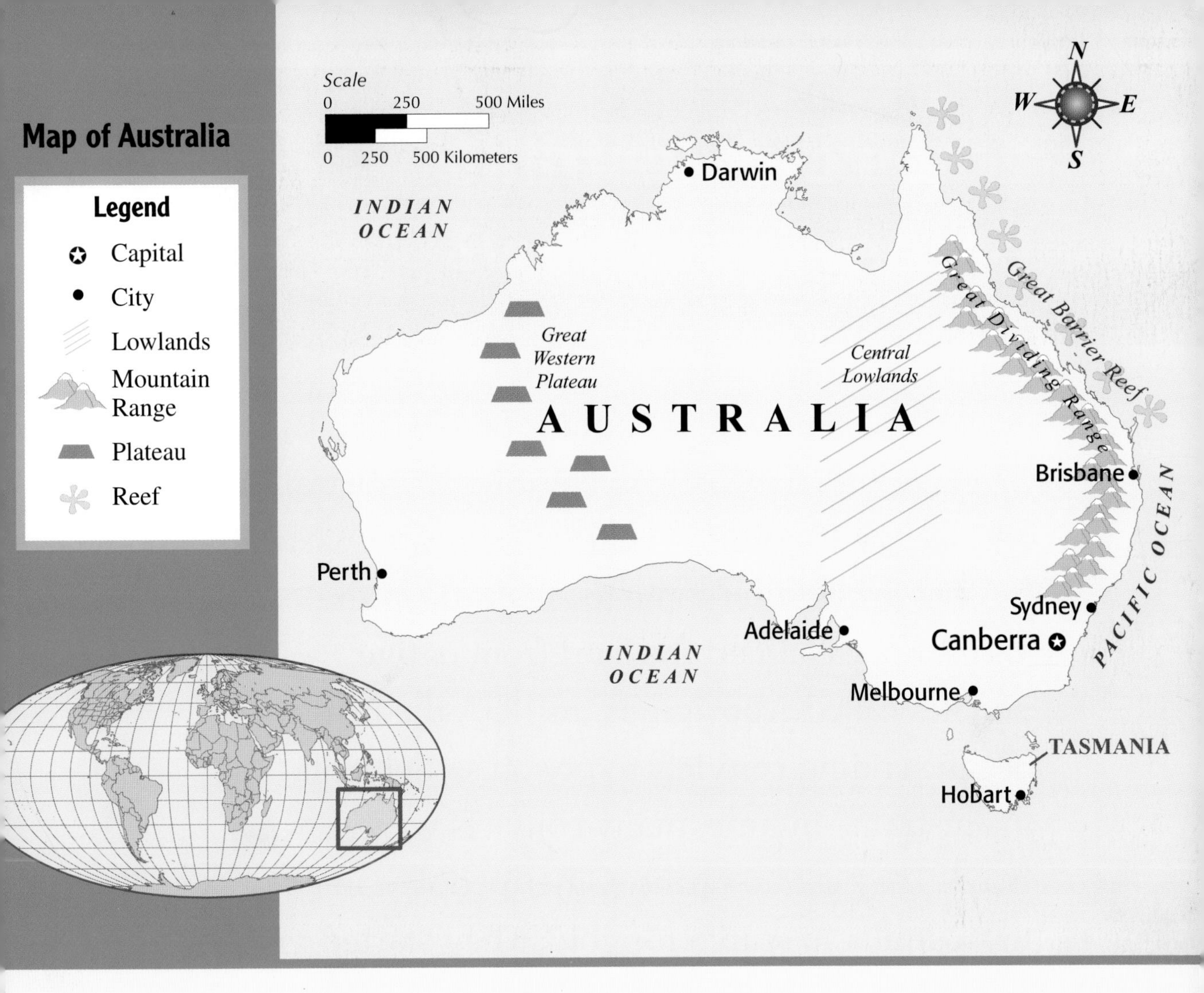

Many landforms stretch across Australia. The mountains of the Great Dividing Range stand along the eastern coast. The Outback is in central and western Australia. Dry deserts and small mountains make up most of the Outback.

When did Australia become a country?

Australia became a country on January 1, 1901. On that date, British **colonies** in Australia became the Commonwealth of Australia.

The British first came to Australia in the 1770s. They claimed the land from native peoples called **Aborigines**. In 1787, the British began sending **convicts** to prison settlements in Australia. In time, many convicts were freed. They set up farms. Other people came to Australia to search for gold. They started colonies with the freed convicts.

Fact!

Aborigines have lived in Australia for at least 50,000 years. They hunted and gathered food. Today, some Aborigines still follow a traditional way of life.

Miners found gold in Coolgarie, Australia, in 1893. It became one of Australia's richest gold fields.

By the 1890s, the colonies wanted to join to form one country. They wrote a **constitution**, which Great Britain approved. British colonies in Australia became states of Australia. Australians named Canberra as the new country's capital.

What type of government does Australia have?

Australia is a **constitutional monarchy**. In 1901, the newly joined colonies made Great Britain's queen the head of state. A **governor general** represents the king or queen in Australia.

Members of **parliament** suggest bills for new laws. A bill becomes law after both the **prime minister** and the governor general sign it. The governor general's signature means the king or queen also approves the law.

Fact!

Australians 18 years and older must vote. Anyone who does not vote can be fined by the government.

Australia's parliament meets to introduce and pass laws.

Australia also has state and territory governments. Australia has six states and two territories, including the island of Tasmania. State and territorial governments make laws on issues like education and **natural resources**.

What kind of housing does Australia have?

Most Australians live in houses or apartments. Houses in cities are often made of brick and have tile roofs. Many houses have yards and a garden.

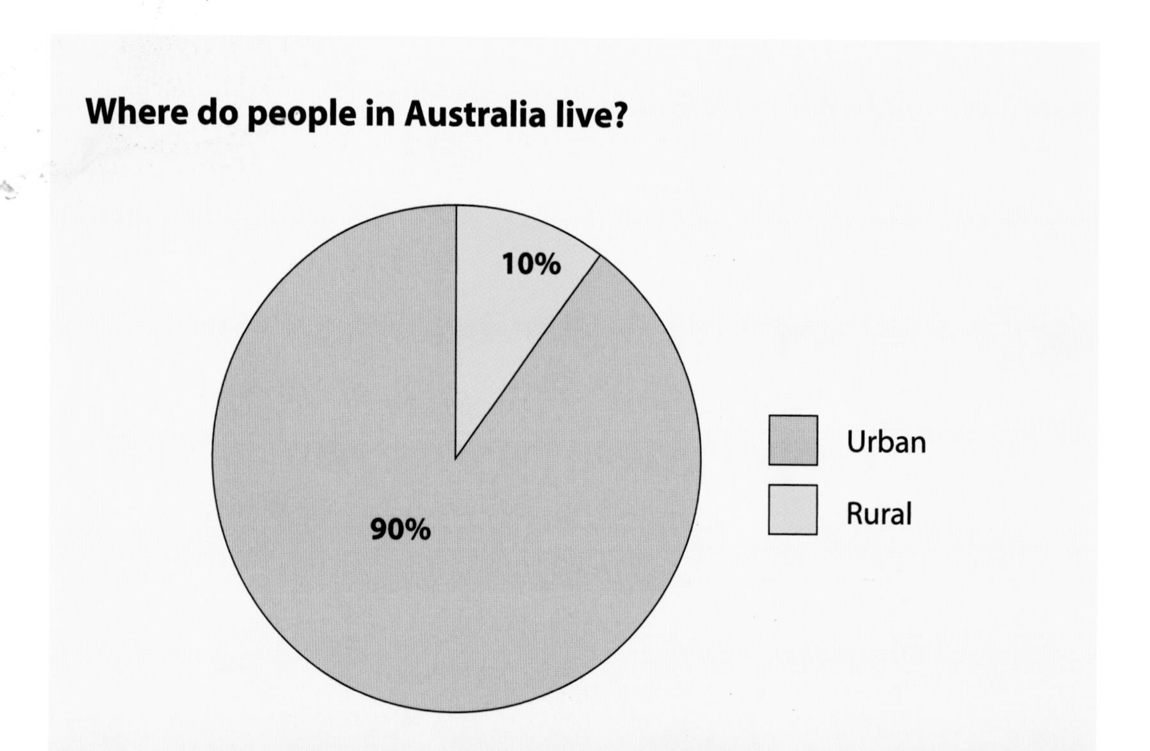

Houses and apartments fill the city of Hobart, Tasmania.

Some Australians live on cattle or sheep stations. Stations are large ranches or farms. They sometimes cover more than 1,000 square miles (2,600 square kilometers). Station houses have areas for an office, a classroom, and guests.

What are Australia's forms of transportation?

Australians travel by car, bus, subway, and taxi. Australia has a good system of paved roads along the coasts. Dirt roads lead into and out of the Outback. Each year, at least 4 million people travel around Sydney on its monorail. In Melbourne, people can catch a ride on cable cars.

Signs remind drivers to watch for camels, wombats, and kangaroos on Australia's roads. ➡

Sydney's monorail gives an overhead view of Darling Harbour.

Australians also travel by train and airplane. Trains carry people and goods. The train ride across Australia from Sydney to Perth takes about two days. Many families on stations own small planes. They fly their planes into town to buy food and supplies.

What are Australia's major industries?

Australia's natural resources support mining. Australians mine coal, gold, and diamonds. They sell some of these minerals to other countries. They also use coal for fuel. They make jewelry and other products with gold and diamonds.

Farming is another major industry. Most farmers raise sheep and cattle. Other farmers grow wheat, sugarcane, and barley. They also grow many fruits, such as peaches, apples, and grapes.

What does Australia import and export?

Imports	*Exports*
computers	*coal*
crude oil	*gold*
machinery	*meat*

Workers pour liquid gold into molds. The gold cools and hardens into gold blocks.

Most Australians work in the service industry. They work in banks, hospitals, and schools. They also work in tourism. Tourists visit the Great Barrier Reef and other natural areas.

What is school like in Australia?

Australian children begin school when they are 6 years old. They must go to school until they are 15 years old. Children study many subjects, including math, history, and science. Most students wear uniforms to school.

Australian grade school students learn about animals that live in their country. ➧

Some "School of the Air" students use computers to do schoolwork.

In the Outback, children often do not live near a school. These children attend the "School of the Air." Students have a classroom at home. They listen to their teachers on the radio. They mail their homework and tests to their teachers.

What are Australia's favorite sports and games?

Australians play and watch many sports. Australians play cricket, soccer, tennis, and basketball. They also hike, surf, and swim. Each year, tennis fans watch the Australian Open in Melbourne.

Many Australians enjoy **rugby**. Rugby is like football. Australians play rugby union, rugby league, and Australian Rules football. Each game has different rules. Australian Rules football is called "footie." Footie is one of Australia's most popular sports.

Fact!

In 1996, track-and-field athlete Cathy Freeman became the first Australian Aborigine to compete in the Olympics.

Australians enjoy a game of Australian Rules football.

Netball is another popular sport in Australia. Netball is a game like basketball. Players can pass but not dribble. They score by shooting the ball through a hoop. The hoop does not have a backboard.

What are the traditional art forms in Australia?

The performing arts are popular in Australia. Australians enjoy going to **operas** and ballets. They also attend plays and musicals. The Sydney Opera House is the busiest art center in the world.

Aborigines are known for their artwork. Some Aborigines make dot paintings. They paint thousands of colored dots to make a picture.

Fact!

Aborigine artists use a stick or nail to apply dots one by one to dot paintings.

An Aborigine man plays a didgeridoo in a traditional ceremony.

Aborigines also play music and dance. They tell stories through their music and dance. Aborigines use many instruments, including the didgeridoo. A didgeridoo looks like a long wooden tube. It makes a low humming noise when played.

What major holidays do people in Australia celebrate?

Australia celebrates two national holidays. January 26 is Australia Day. On this day, people celebrate the first British colony in Australia. They watch fireworks and attend parades. April 25 is ANZAC Day. ANZAC stands for Australia New Zealand Army Corps. On this day, Australians remember soldiers who served in wars.

Christians in Australia celebrate Christmas. During Christmas the weather is hot. Families have a barbecue or go to the beach.

What other holidays do people in Australia celebrate?

Boxing Day
Commonwealth Day
Easter
New Year's Day
Queen's Birthday

Australia is warm in December. People often head to the beach to celebrate Christmas.

Aborigine festivals are called corroborees (kuh-RO-buh-reez). Aborigines honor their culture through music and dance. Dancers paint their bodies. Musicians play the didgeridoo and beat drums.

What are the traditional foods of Australia?

Australians eat many of the same foods as people in Great Britain. Australians call breakfast "brekkie." For brekkie, some Australians eat eggs, sausage, or cereal. Others eat toast with baked beans or spaghetti. For lunch, they eat fish and chips, meat pies, or sausage rolls. For dinner they eat meat with vegetables. Australians also often eat foods from other countries, such as Greece, Italy, and China.

Fact!

Aborigines living in the Outback sometimes eat grubs, wild grasses, and kangaroo tails. These foods are called bush tucker.

Most people spread Vegemite on toast for a snack.

People also enjoy eating Australian foods. They make sponge cakes called Lamingtons. These cakes are covered with chocolate and coconut. Australians also eat Vegemite, a salty black spread made from yeast.

What is family life like in Australia?

Family life in Australia is like family life in North America. Most children live with both of their parents. Others live with one parent or with relatives.

On weekends, families enjoy the outdoors. They watch and play sports. They also have barbecues in their backyard or at the beach.

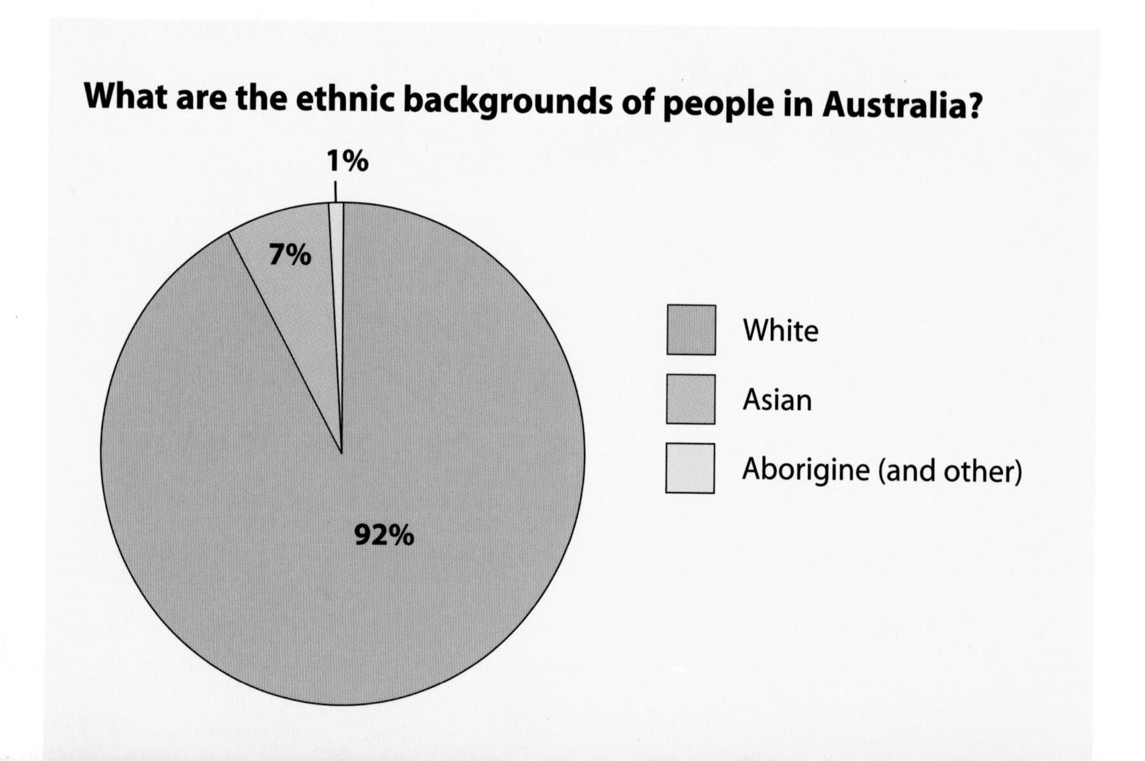

An Australian family enjoys a picnic near a stream.

Aborigine families used to live in rural areas. They would travel to find food and water. Today, many Aborigine families live, work, and go to school in or near cities.

Australia Fast Facts

Official name:

Commonwealth of Australia

Population:

19,913,144 people

Land area:

2,967,893 square miles (7,686,843 square kilometers)

Capital city:

Canberra

Average annual precipitation (Sydney):

48 inches (122 centimeters)

Language:

English

Average January temperature (Sydney):

73 degrees Fahrenheit (23 degrees Celsius)

Natural resources:

coal, diamonds, gold, uranium

Average July temperature (Sydney):

53 degrees Fahrenheit (12 degrees Celsius)

Religions:

Anglican	*26%*
Roman Catholic	*26%*
Other Christian	*24%*
Non-Christian	*11%*
Other	*13%*

Money and Flag

Money:

Australia's money is the Australian dollar. In 2004, 1 U.S. dollar equaled 1.4 Australian dollars. One Canadian dollar equaled 1.04 Australian dollars.

Flag:

The Australian flag has the flag of the United Kingdom in the upper left side. A large seven-pointed star is in the lower left side. Australians call this star the Commonwealth Star. It stands for the original Australian colonies. The other stars are in the same pattern as the Southern Cross constellation.

Learn to Speak Australian English

People in Australia often use different words for everyday things than people in the United States do. Below are some words used in Australia.

American	*Australian*	*Pronunciation*
hello	g'day	(guh-DAY)
thank you	ta	(TAH)
friend	mate	(MATE)
man	bloke	(BLOUK)
woman	sheila	(SHE-lah)
food	tucker	(TUK-eh)

Glossary

Aborigine (ab-uh-RIJ-uh-nee)—one of the native peoples of Australia; Aborigines lived in Australia before Europeans arrived.

colony (KOL-uh-nee)—a large area that has been settled by people from another country

constitution (kon-stuh-TOO-shuhn)—the written system of laws in a country that states the rights of the people and the powers of government

constitutional monarchy (kon-sti-TOO-shuhn-uhl MON-ar-kee)—a system of government in which the monarch's powers are limited

convict (KON-vikt)—someone who is in prison because he or she has committed a crime

governor general (GUHV-urn-ur JEN-ur-uhl)—a leader chosen to represent the king or queen as leader of a country

natural resource (NACH-ur-uhl REE-sorss)—a material found in nature that is useful to people

opera (OP-ur-uh)—a play in which all or most of the words are sung

parliament (PAR-luh-muhnt)—the group of people who have been elected to make the laws in some countries

prime minister (PRIME MIN-uh-stur)—the person in charge of a government in some countries

rugby (RUHG-bee)—a form of football played by two teams that kick, pass, and carry an oval ball

Internet Sites

FactHound offers a safe, fun way to find Internet sites related to this book. All of the sites on FactHound have been researched by our staff.

Here's how:

1. Visit *www.facthound.com*
2. Type in this special code **0736837477** for age-appropriate sites. Or enter a search word related to this book for a more general search.
3. Click on the **Fetch It** button.

FactHound will fetch the best sites for you!

Read More

Gray, Shirley W. *Australia.* First Reports. Minneapolis: Compass Point Books, 2001.

Rose, Elizabeth. *A Primary Source Guide to Australia.* Countries of the World, a Primary Source Journey. New York: PowerKids Press, 2004.

Somervill, Barbara A. *Australia.* Geography of the World Series. Chanhassen, Minn.: Child's World, 2004.

Striveildi, Cheryl. *Australia.* A Buddy Book. Edina, Minn.: Abdo, 2003.

Index